His
Little Instruction
Book For Your Life,
Home & Job

HIS LITTLE INSTRUCTION BOOK
For Your Life, Home & Job

Compiled and Written By:
Michael Q. Pink

Cover Design By:
Herron Largent Digital Studios

Introduction

In 1985, four years after a failed marriage, a failed business, the recent death of my first born child, and the very painful loss of all communication with my surviving children Ryan and Amy, I could only conclude that I had in fact failed at life itself.

Then one day, when in anguished desperation I cried out to the Lord for help, He very lovingly guided me into His word and gave me a light for my path. I vowed to Him that day, that I would do all that His word said for me to do, if He would do all that His word said He would do. If

He fulfilled His word as revealed in the Bible, then I would tell everyone. If he did not, then how could I tell anyone? As I read His word and followed His wisdom, my life began to make sense again. He redeemed my past, made sense of my present and gave me hope for the future.

In 1988, I began to fulfill my promise to Him by writing *"The Bible Incorporated,"* a conversational compilation of Scripture pertaining to 101 work, business and life related topics. It went on to become a national best seller with approximately 250,000 copies in print. That success led to many church and business seminars where I "tell everyone" how God keeps His promises.

◆ INTRODUCTION ◆

From that best selling book I have taken some of the most loved passages of conversational Scripture and arranged them under numerous topics of interest so that you too may experience the God who makes and *keeps* His promises.

When you have drunk from the wells of living water, nothing else will satisfy.

For Ryan and Amy

So much to say, but words still fail.
Tears shed at night, behind a veil.

Destiny awaits, morning has come.
The future is yours, bright as the sun.

I LOVE YOU

Keep your tongue from evil, and your lips from speaking guile,[1] for there is not a word in your tongue, that the Lord doesn't know it already.[2]

A man of great wrath will suffer punishment.[3]

1

1) Psalms 34:13   2) Psalms 139:4   3) Proverbs 19:19

2

So let every man be swift to hear, slow to speak, slow to wrath: for the wrath of man does not work the righteousness of God.[1]

You are snared and taken with the words of your mouth.[2]

1) James 1:19,20   2) Proverbs 6:2

He that is slow to anger,[1] or wrath is of great understanding,[2] better than the mighty,[1] and knows that a soft answer turns away wrath; grievous words only stir up anger.[3]

3

1) Proverbs 16:32   2) Proverbs 14:29   3) Proverbs 15:1

4

He that is soon angry, deals foolishly,[1] but he that keeps his mouth and controls his tongue, keeps his soul from troubles.[2]

Death and life are in the power of the tongue; and they that love it shall eat the fruit thereof.[3]

1) Proverbs 14:17   2) Proverbs 21:23   3) Proverbs 18:21

Cease from anger, forsake wrath,[1] take heed to your ways that you don't sin with your tongue, and keep your mouth with a bridle while the wicked are before you.[2]

5

1) Psalms 37:8 2) Psalms 39:1

6

With the tongue we bless God, even the Father; and with it we curse men, which are made in the likeness of God. Out of the same mouth proceeds blessing and cursing. These things should not be so.[1]

1) James 3:9,10

Remember, he that will love life, and see good days, let him refrain his tongue from evil, and his lips that they speak no guile.[1]

Vengeance is mine, I will repay, says the Lord.[2]

7

1) 1 Peter 3:10   2) Hebrews 10:30

BURN OUT

8

The Lord gives power to the faint: and to them that have no might, He increases strength.[1] But they that wait upon the Lord shall renew their strength, mount up with wings as eagles, run and not be weary, walk and not faint.[2]

1) Isaiah 40:29   2) Isaiah 40:31

Submit yourself therefore to God,[1] casting all your care upon Him, for He cares for you,[2] and resist the devil, and he will flee from you.[1]

What shall we say then? If God be for us, who can be against us?[3]

9

1) James 4:7   2) 1 Peter 5:7   3) Romans 8:31

10

Be confident of this very thing, that He which has begun a good work in you, will perform it until the day of Jesus Christ.[1] For it is God which works in you both to will and to do of His good pleasure.[2]

1) Philippians 1:6   2) Philippians 2:13

BURN OUT

L ook unto Jesus, the author and finisher of our faith; who for the joy that was set before Him, endured the cross, despising the shame, and is set down at the right hand of the throne of God.[1]

11

1) Hebrews 12:2

12

The Lord is my shepherd; I shall not want, He makes me to lie down in green pastures; He leads me beside the still waters. He restores my soul,[1] for there remains a rest for the people of God.[2]

1) Psalm 23:1-3   2) Hebrews 4:9

BURN OUT

You prepare a table before me in the presence of my enemies; You anoint my head with oil; my cup runs over. Surely goodness and mercy shall follow me all the days of my life, and I will dwell in the house of the Lord forever.[1]

13

1) Psalms 23:5,6

14

The Lord increases His people greatly; making them stronger than their enemies,[1] and he that has clean hands will be stronger and stronger.[2]

1) Psalms 105:24   2) Job 17:9

BURN OUT

God satisfies your mouth with good things, so that your youth is renewed like the eagles;[1] and when you walk in the midst of trouble, He will revive you.[2]

15

1) Psalms 103:5   2) Psalms 138:7

BURN OUT

16

The Lord is with them that are of a contrite and humble spirit, to revive the spirit of the humble and to revive the heart of the contrite ones.[1] So wait on the Lord,[2] be of good courage, and He will strengthen your heart,[3] according to His word.[4]

1) Isaiah 57:15   2) Psalms 27:14   3) Psalms 31:24   4) Psalms 119:28

Come to Me, all you that labor and are heavy laden, and I will give you rest. Take My yoke upon you, and learn from Me; for I am meek and lowly in heart, and you will find rest for your souls.[1]

17

1) Matthew 11:28,29

CONFIDENCE

18

In the fear of the Lord is strong confidence.[1] Let us therefore come boldly unto the throne of grace, that we may obtain mercy, and find grace to help in time of need,[2] for the Lord shall be your confidence.[3]

1) Proverbs 14:26   2) Hebrews 4:16   3) Proverbs 3:26

CONFIDENCE

You are of God, and greater is He that is in you than he that is in the world.[1]

Cast not away your confidence, which has great recompense of reward. For you have need of patience, that after you have done the will of God, you will receive the promise.[2]

19

1) 1 John 4:4   2) Hebrews 10:35,36

CONFIDENCE

20

Be confident of this very thing, that He which has begun a good work in you will perform it until the day of Jesus Christ.[1]

1) Philippians 1:6

CONFIDENCE

The Lord is my helper, and I will not fear what man shall do unto me.[1] For by Him I have run through a troop; and by my God I have leaped over a wall.[2]

21

1) Hebrews 13:6   2) Psalms 18:29

CONFIDENCE

22

A nd this is the confidence that we have in Him, that if we ask anything according to His will, He hears us, whatever we ask, we know that we have the petitions that we desired of Him.[1]

1) 1 John 5:14,15

CONFIDENCE

Not by might, nor by power, but by My Spirit says the Lord.[1]

23

It is better to trust in the Lord than to put confidence in man.[2]

1) Zechariah 4:6   2) Psalms 118:8

24

For if our heart condemns us, God is greater than our heart, and knows all things. If our heart does not condemn us, then we have confidence toward God, and receive from Him whatever we ask, because we obey His commands and do what pleases Him.[1]

1) 1 John 3:20-22

We are more than conquerors through Him that loved us,[1] and we can do all things through Christ who strengthens us;[2] in whom we have boldness and access with confidence through faith in Him.[3]

25

1) Romans 8:37   2) Philippians 4:13   3) Ephesians 3:12

CRISIS

26

As for me, I will call upon God; and the Lord will save me,[1] for the Lord is near to them that call upon Him, to all that call upon Him in truth.[2]

1) Psalms 55:16   2) Psalms 145:18

CRISIS

C all upon the Lord in your day of trouble,[1] and He will hear you,[2] answer you and[1] deliver you[3] from all your fears,[4] honor you[3] and save you from all your troubles.[2]

27

1) Psalms 86:7   2) Psalms 34:6   3) Psalms 91:15   4) Psalms 34:4

CRISIS

28

For though you walk in the midst of trouble, He will revive you; He will stretch forth His hand against the wrath of your enemies, and His right hand will save you.[1]

1) Psalms 138:7

CRISIS

Put on the whole armor of God, that you may be able to stand against the schemes of the devil.[1] Yes, submit yourself to God. Resist the devil and he will flee from you,[2] and having done all, stand.[3]

29

1) Ephesians 6:11   2) James 4:7   3) Ephesians 6:13

30

When you pass through the waters,
God will be with you; and
through the rivers, they will not
overflow you. When you walk through
the fire, you will not be burned, neither
will the flame kindle upon you.[1]

1) Isaiah 43:2

CRISIS

The weapons of our warfare are not carnal, but mighty through God to the pulling down of strongholds.[1]

No weapon formed against you will prosper and every tongue that rises against you in judgement, you will condemn.[2]

31

1) 2 Corinthians 10:4   2) Isaiah 54:17

CRISIS

The Lord is your hiding place. He will preserve you from trouble; He will compass you about with songs of deliverance,[1] and the angel of the Lord will encamp round about them that fear Him, and deliver them.[2]

32

1) Psalms 32:7   2) Psalms 34:7

So cast all your care upon Him, for He cares for you,[1] and is the source of your help.[2] His way is perfect, the word of the Lord is tried and true; He is a shield to all those that trust in Him.[3]

33

1) 1 Peter 5:7   2) Psalms 121:2   3) Psalms 18:30

34

The Lord will teach and instruct
you in the way you should go,
guiding you with His eye.[1] Be wise and
listen to His counsel,[2] for it will
guide you[3] and stand forever.[4]

1) Psalms 32:8   2) Proverbs 12:15   3) Psalms 73:24   4) Psalms 33:11

Make His testimonies your delight, and they will counsel you.[1] Yes, God's word is a lamp for your feet and a light for your path.[2] So apply your heart to instruction and your ears to the words of knowledge.[3]

35

1) Psalms 119:24   2) Psalms 119:105   3) Proverbs 23:12

DECISIONS

36

The Lord will show you the path of life;[1] Simply commit your works to the Lord and your thoughts will be established.[2] Though your heart devises a plan, the Lord will direct your steps.[3]

1) Psalms 16:11   2) Proverbs 16:3   3) Proverbs 16:9

Without counsel, the people fall,[1]
and purposes are disappointed,[2]
but in the multitude of counsellors there is
safety[1] and every purpose is established.[2]

37

1) Proverbs 11:14   2) Proverbs 15:22

DECISIONS

38

Only with good advice[1] and wise counsel should you make plans to war,[2] and don't seek the counsel of ungodly or wicked people.[3]

1) Proverbs 20:18   2) Proverbs 24:6   3) Psalms 1:1

Trust in the Lord with all your heart and lean not to your own understanding. In all your ways acknowledge Him, and He will direct your paths.[1]

39

Bless the Lord who gives you counsel and instructs you at night with your heart.[2]

1) Proverbs 3:5,6   2) Psalms 16:7

The Lord will teach you to profit, lead you by the way you should go,[1] and direct your work in truth.[2]

As the heavens are higher than the earth, so are His ways higher than your ways and His thoughts than your thoughts.[3]

40

1) Isaiah 48:17   2) Isaiah 61:8   3) Isaiah 55:9

DECISIONS

Remember that a man's life is not his own; It is not for man to direct his steps.[1] So seek the Lord early, thirsting and longing for Him,[2] and the Lord will help you, and you will not be confounded. Set your face like a flint, and you will not be ashamed.[3]

41

1) Jeremiah 10:23   2) Psalms 63:1   3) Isaiah 50:7

DECISIONS

I f you lack wisdom, ask of God who gives to all men liberally and without finding fault and it will be given to you; only ask in faith.[1]

42

G od is not the author of confusion, but of peace.[2]

1) James 1:5,6   2) 1 Corinthians 14:33

DEPRESSION

B lessed are you that weep now; for you shall laugh,[1] for the Lord has appointed unto you the oil of joy for mourning, the garment of praise for the spirit of heaviness, that you might be called trees of righteousness, the planting of the Lord, that He might be glorified.[2]

43

1) Luke 6:21   2) Isaiah 61:3

DEPRESSION

44

Remove sorrow from your heart,[1] and do not let it be troubled; neither let it be afraid.[2] You believe in God, believe also in Jesus,[3] being confident of this very thing, that He which began a good work in you will perform it until the day of Jesus Christ.[4]

1) Ecclesiastes 11:10   2) John 14:27   3) John 14:1   4) Philippians 1:6

DEPRESSION

Hope in God,[1] remember Him,[2] and praise Him who is the health of your countenance and your God,[1] for it is God which is at work in you, both to will and to do of His good pleasure.[3]

45

1) Psalms 42:11   2) Psalms 42:6   3) Philippians 2:13

DEPRESSION

46

Rejoice in the Lord always, and again I say rejoice.[1] In everything give thanks for this is the will of God in Christ Jesus concerning you.[2]

1) Philippians 4:4   2) 1 Thessalonians 5:18

Our light affliction, which is but for a moment, works for us a far more exceeding and eternal weight of glory.[1] But remember, weeping may endure for a night, but joy comes in the morning.[2]

47

1) 2 Corinthians 4:17   2) Psalms 30:5

DEPRESSION

48

Beloved, think it not strange concerning the fiery trial which is to try you, as though some strange thing happened to you: but rejoice that you partake in the sufferings of Christ, that you may be full of joy when His glory is revealed.[1]

1) 1 Peter 4:12,13

Firmly understand that neither death, nor life, nor angels, nor principalities, nor powers, nor things present, nor things to come, nor height, nor depth, nor any other creature shall be able to separate us from the love of God which is in Christ Jesus our Lord.[1]

49

1) Romans 8:38,39

50

Finally, whatever is true, whatever is noble, whatever is just, whatever is pure, whatever is lovely, whatever is of good report; if there is any virtue, if there is any praise, think on these things.[1]

1) Philippians 4:8

DISAPPOINTMENT

Rejoice greatly, though now for a season, if need be, you are in heaviness through many trials; that the trial |51| of your faith, being much more precious than gold that perishes, though it be tried with fire, might be found unto praise and honor at the appearing of Jesus Christ.[1]

1) 1 Peter 1:6,7

DISAPPOINTMENT

52

Do not let your heart be troubled,[1] though you walk in the midst of trouble, God will revive you.[2]

Be of good courage, and He will strengthen your heart, all you that hope in the Lord,[3] for He has promised to never leave you nor forsake you.[4]

DISAPPOINTMENT

Pray without ceasing, in everything give thanks; for this is the will of God in Christ Jesus concerning you.[1]

53

The eye of the Lord is upon them that fear Him,[2] and He takes pleasure in them that hope in His mercy.[3]

1) 1 Thessalonians 5:17,18   2) Psalms 33:18   3) Psalms 147:11

DISAPPOINTMENT

54

We are troubled on every side, yet not distressed; we are perplexed, but not in despair; persecuted, but not forsaken; cast down, but not destroyed.[1]

Cast not away your confidence for it will be richly rewarded.[2]

1) 2 Corinthians 4:8,9   2) Hebrews 10:35

FAITH

N ow faith comes by hearing, and hearing by the Word of God,[1] being the substance of things hoped for, the evidence of things not seen.[2]

55

1) Romans 10:17   2) Hebrews 11:1

FAITH

56

Without faith, it is impossible to please God for He that comes to God must believe that He is, and that He is a rewarder of them that diligently seek Him.[1] Let us therefore come boldly to the throne of grace, that we may obtain mercy, and find grace in time of need.[2]

1) Hebrews 11:6   2) Hebrews 4:16

FAITH

In times past, men of God through faith, subdued kingdoms, wrought righteousness, obtained promises, stopped the mouths of lions, quenched the violence of fire, escaped the edge of the sword, out of weakness were made strong, waxed valiant in fight, turned to flight the armies of the aliens.[1]

57

1) Hebrews 11:33,34

FAITH

58

God has dealt to every man the measure of faith,[1] that we might become the children of God through faith in Jesus Christ.[2] For by grace are you saved through faith; and that not of yourselves: it is the gift of God.[3]

1) Romans 12:3   2) Galatians 3:26   3) Ephesians 2:8

FAITH

So let us hold fast the profession of our faith without wavering; for He is faithful that promised.[1] Now the just shall live by faith: but if any man draws back, the Lord will have no pleasure in him.[2]

59

1) Hebrews 10:23   2) Hebrews 10:38

60

So take the shield of faith with which you can quench all the fiery darts of the wicked one,[1] and the whole armor of God,[2] and fight the good fight of faith, laying hold of eternal life,[3] that Christ may dwell in your hearts by faith.[4]

1) Ephesians 6:16   2) Ephesians 6:1   3) 1 Timothy 6:12   4) Ephesians 3:17

Have faith in God,[1] and it will save you,[2] make you whole,[3] and whatever things you desire when you pray, believe that you receive them, and you will have them.[4]

61

1) Mark 11:22   2) Luke 7:50   3) Luke 8:48   4) Mark 11:24

62

Build yourself up on your most holy faith, praying in the Holy Ghost,[1] for we walk by faith and not by sight,[2] and all things, whatsoever you ask in prayer believing, you shall receive.[3]

1) Jude 1:20   2) 2 Corinthians 5:7   3) Matthew 21:22

FAVOR

Let mercy and truth never leave you; bind them around your neck; write them on the table of your heart. Then you will find favor and good understanding in the sight of God and man.[1]

63

1) Proverbs 3:3,4

FAVOR

64

The Lord will bless the righteous and surround him like a shield with favor.[1] In His favor is life,[2] making you steady as a mountain.[3]

O taste and see that the Lord is good, and blessed is the man that trusts in Him.[4]

1) Psalms 5:12   2) Psalms 30:5   3) Psalms 30:7   4) Psalms 34:8

FAVOR

Whoever finds wisdom, finds life, and shall obtain favor of the Lord.[1]

He that diligently seeks good, finds favor,[2] for a good man obtains favor of the Lord.[3]

65

---

1) Proverbs 8:35   2) Proverbs 11:27   3) Proverbs 12:2

66

How precious are God's thoughts towards you; How great is the sum of them![1] Whoever touches you, touches the apple of His eye,[2] for great is His mercy toward you.[3]

Among the righteous, there is favor.[4]

1) Psalms 24:4,5   2) Psalms 139:17   3) Zechariah 2:8   4) Proverbs 14:9

GOALS

Forget those things which are behind, and reach forward to those things which are ahead, pressing toward the mark for the prize of the high calling of God in Christ Jesus.[1]

67

1) Philippians 3:13,14

68

Make the very most of time,
seizing every opportunity,
behaving wisely,[1] redeeming the time
because the days are evil.[2]

Do not be unwise, but understand
what the will of the Lord is.[3]

1) Colossians 4:5   2) Ephesians 5:16   3) Ephesians 5:17

Hope deferred makes the heart sick; but when the desire comes, it is a tree of life.[1]

69

And whatever things you desire when you pray, believe that you receive them and you shall have them.[2]

1) Proverbs 13:12   2) Mark 11:24

70

Write the vision, and make it plain upon tablets that he may run that reads it.[1] For where there is no vision, the people perish;[2] but a dream comes through the multitude of business.[3]

1) Habakkuk 2:2   2) Proverbs 29:18   3) Ecclesiastes 5:3

D elight yourself in the Lord, and He will give you the desires of your heart.[1] Yes, He will fulfill the desire of them that fear Him.[2]

71

1) Psalms 37:4   2) Psalms 145:19

72

The desire of the righteous is only good,[1] and shall be granted,[2] and when it is accomplished it is sweet to the soul.[3]

Through desire a man, having separated himself, seeks and intermeddles with all wisdom.[4]

1) Proverbs 11:23   2) Proverbs 10:24   3) Proverbs 13:19   4) Proverbs 18:1

GOALS

God knows the desire of the humble; He will prepare their heart and cause their ear to hear.[1] For their desire is before God;[2] He will give them their heart's desire and not withhold the request of their lips.[3]

73

1) Psalms 10:17   2) Psalms 38:9   3) Psalms 21:2

GOSSIP

74

A gossip goes around revealing secrets.[1] The rumors they spread are like dainty morsels, going down into the innermost parts of the belly,[2] therefore, don't meddle with him that flatters with his lips.[3]

1) Proverbs 11:13   2) Proverbs 26:22   3) Proverbs 20:19

GOSSIP

Where no wood is, the fire goes out, so where there is no gossip, the strife ceases.[1]

75

Speak no evil of any man, be gentle, showing all meekness unto all men,[2] for a wholesome tongue is a tree of life.[3]

1) Proverbs 26:20   2) Titus 3:2   3) Proverbs 15:4

In the multitude of words, there is no sin lacking, but he that refrains his lips is wise.[1]

Simply let your "Yes" be "Yes," and your "No," be "No." For whatever is more than this comes from the evil one.[2]

76

1) Proverbs 10:19   2) Matthew 5:37

Don't be afraid, for God is with you: Don't be dismayed for He is your God: He will strengthen you, yes He will help you and uphold you with the right hand of His righteousness.[1]

77

1) Isaiah 41:10

78

Wait on the Lord and be of good courage and He will strengthen your heart: Wait I say on the Lord,[1] for there is a rest to the people of God.[2]

1) Psalms 27:14   2) Hebrews 4:9

HOPELESS

Be confident of this very thing, that He which began a good work in you will perform it until the day of Jesus Christ,[1] for it is God which works in you both to will and to do of His good pleasure.[2]

79

1) Philippians 1:6   2) Philippians 2:13

HOPELESS

The battle is not yours but God's,[1] so look unto Jesus, the author and finisher of your faith,[2] and say to the mountain facing you, "Be removed and cast into the sea," not doubting in your heart, but believing that those things that you say will come to pass.[3]

80

1) 2 Chronicles 20:15   2) Hebrews 12:2   3) Mark 11:23

If you have run with the footmen, and they have wearied you, then how can you contend with horses?[1]

Be strengthened according to God's word.[2] He will never leave you nor forsake you.[3] He is with you always, even unto the end of the world.[4]

1) Jeremiah 12:5   2) Psalms 119:28   3) Hebrews 13:5   4) Matthew 28:20

HOPELESS

82

Be not slothful, but followers of them who through faith and patience inherit the promises.[1] Say of the Lord, He is my refuge and my fortress; my God in whom I will trust.[2]

1) Hebrews 6:12   2) Psalms 91:2

Press toward the mark for the prize of the high calling of God in Christ Jesus,[1] not being weary in well doing; for in due season you will reap, if you don't faint and give up.[2]

83

1) Philippians 3:14   2) Galatians 6:9

Wealth makes many friends; but the poor is separated from his neighbor.[1] The poor man pleads for mercy,[2] and is hated even by his own neighbor, but the rich man has many friends,[3] and answers roughly.[2]

84

1) Proverbs 19:4   2) Proverbs 18:23   3) Proverbs 14:20

For the love of money is the root of all evil: which while some coveted after, they have erred from the faith, and pierced themselves through with many sorrows.[1]

85

1) 1 Timothy 6:10

86

Owe no man anything, but to love one another,[1] for the rich rules over the poor and the borrower is servant to the lender.[2]

Don't withhold good from those who deserve it, when it's in your power to take action.[3]

1) Romans 13:8   2) Proverbs 22:7   3) Proverbs 3:27

B lessed is he that considers the poor:
The Lord will deliver him in the day
of trouble.[1]

87

I t is a sore evil when riches are kept just
for the owners, to their own hurt.[2]

1) Psalms 41:1   2) Ecclesiastes 5:13

88

So charge them that are rich in this world, that they be not highminded, nor trust in uncertain riches; but in the living God who gives us richly all things to enjoy.[1] For people who want to be rich fall into temptation and a snare, and into many foolish and hurtful lusts which draw men into destruction and ruin.[2]

1) 1 Timothy 6:17   2) 1 Timothy 6:9

PATIENCE

Know this, that the trying of your faith works patience, but let patience have her perfect work, that you may be perfect and entire, lacking nothing.[1]

89

1) James 1:3,4

90

For you have need of patience, that after you have done the will of God, you might receive the promise.[1] So don't be slothful, but followers of them who through faith and patience inherit the promises.[2]

1) Hebrews 10:36   2) Hebrews 6:12

Wait on the Lord, be of good courage,[1] waiting patiently for Him,[2] keeping His way,[3] and He will strengthen your heart,[1] exalt you to inherit the land and give you meat in due season.[4]

91

1) Psalms 27:14   2) Psalms 37:7   3) Psalms 37:34   4) Psalms 145:15

PATIENCE

92

Glory also in your tribulations,
knowing that tribulation works
patience; and patience, experience;
and experience, hope; and hope won't
make you ashamed.[1]

1) Romans 5:3-5

PATIENCE

The patient in spirit is better than the proud in spirit,[1] so be patient; establish your heart, for the coming of the Lord draws near,[2] and after you have patiently endured, you will obtain the promise.[3]

93

1) Ecclesiastes 7:8   2) James 5:8   3) Hebrews 6:15

94

Wherefore, seeing we also are compassed about with so great a cloud of witnesses, let us lay aside every weight, and the sin which does so easily beset us, and let us run with patience the race that is set before us.[1]

1) Hebrews 12:1

The fruit of the Spirit is love, joy, peace, patience, kindness, goodness, faith, gentleness and self control.[1]

95

Wait on your God continually,[2] for He is the God of your salvation and He will hear you.[3]

1) Galatians 5:22   2) Hosea 12:6   3) Micah 7:7

96

Be not weary well doing,[1] for God has satiated the weary soul, and has replenished every sorrowful soul.[2] Men ought always to pray, and not to faint,[3] though our outward man perish, the inward man is renewed day by day.[4]

1) 2 Thessalonians 3:13   2) Jeremiah 31:25   3) Luke 18:1   4) 2 Corinthians 4:16

PERSEVERANCE

Only be strong and very courageous that you may observe to do according to all the law which Moses, God's servant commanded you: turn not from it to the right hand or to the left, that you may prosper wherever you go.[1]

97

1) Joshua 1:7

PERSEVERANCE

98

Turn to your God: keep mercy and judgement, and wait on your God continually,[1] and He will renew your strength, you will mount up with wings as eagles; you will run and not be weary; you will walk and not faint.[2]

1) Hosea 12:6   2) Isaiah 40:31

PERSEVERANCE

Continue in the things which you have learned and have been assured of,[1] praying always with all prayer and supplication in the Spirit, being mindful to this end with all perseverance and supplication for all the saints.[2]

99

1) 2 Timothy 3:14   2) Ephesians 6:18

PERSEVERANCE

100

Jesus will present you holy and unblamable and unreprovable in His sight if you continue in the faith grounded and settled, and be not moved away from the hope of the gospel, which you have heard.[1]

1) Colossians 1:22,23

PERSEVERANCE

Continue in the faith, for it is through much tribulation that we must enter into the kingdom of God.[1] So continue in prayer, watch in thanksgiving,[2] and don't be weary in well doing: for in due season you will reap, if you faint not.[3]

101

1) Acts 14:22   2) Colossians 4:2   3) Galatians 6:9

PRAYER

102

Our Father which art in heaven. Hallowed be thy name. Thy kingdom come. Thy will be done in earth, as in heaven. Give us this day our daily bread. Forgive us our debts, as we forgive our debtors. Lead us not into temptation, but deliver us from evil: For thine is the kingdom, the power and the glory forever.[1]

1) Matthew 6:10-13

Pray that you enter not into temptation,[1] and when you don't know how to pray, the Spirit will also help you in your weakness, making intercession for you with groanings which cannot be uttered.[2]

103

1) Luke 22:40   2) Romans 8:26

104

Men everywhere ought to pray, lifting up holy hands, without wrath and doubting,[1] for he that is doubtful is like a wave of the sea driven and tossed. Let not that man think he will receive anything of the Lord.[2]

1) 1 Timothy 2:8   2) James 1:6,7

When you pray, enter into your closet, and when you have shut your door, pray to your Father which is in secret; and your Father which sees in secret will reward you openly.[1]

105

1) Matthew 6:6

PRAYER

106

And when you stand praying, forgive, if you have ought against any, that your Father in heaven may also forgive you your trespasses.[1]

Pray without ceasing.[2]

1) Mark 11:25   2) 1 Thessalonians 5:17

PRAYER

The eyes of the Lord are over the righteous and His ears are open to their prayers.[1] Yes, the effectual fervent prayer of a righteous man avails much.[2]

107

1) 1 Peter 3:12   2) James 5:16

PRAYER

108

If God's people which are called by His name, will humble themselves and pray, and seek His face, and turn from their wicked ways; then He will hear from heaven, and will forgive their sin, and will heal their land.[1]

1) 2 Chronicles 7:14

PRAYER

Continue in prayer,[1] for we have this confidence in God, that if we ask anything according to His will, He hears us, and if we know that He hears us, whatever we ask, we know that we have the petitions that we desired of Him.[2]

109

1) Colossians 4:2   2) 1 John 5:14,15

110

Pray always with all prayer and supplication in the Spirit,[1] being careful for nothing; but in everything by prayer and supplication with thanksgiving, let your requests be made known to God.[2]

1) Ephesians 6:18   2) Philippians 4:6

PROMOTION

Promotion comes neither from the east, nor the west, nor from the south, but God is the judge. He puts one down and exalts another.[1]

Exalt and embrace wisdom and she will promote and honor you.[2]

111

1) Psalms 75:6,7   2) Proverbs 4:8

PROMOTION

112

Humble yourself therefore under the mighty hand of God,[1] in His sight,[2] that He may lift you up,[1] and exalt you in due time.[2] For God resists the proud, but gives grace to the humble.[3]

1) 1 Peter 5:6   2) James 4:10   3) James 4:6

PROMOTION

Whoever will exalt himself will be humbled, but whoever will humble himself will be exalted.[1]

Exalt and embrace wisdom and she will promote you and honor you.[2]

113

1) Matthew 23:12   2) Proverbs 4:8

PROMOTION

114

The fear of the Lord will instruct you in wisdom; and humility goes before honor.[1] In fact, it is humility and the fear of the Lord that bring wealth and honor and life.[2]

1) Proverbs 15:33   2) Proverbs 22:4

Wait on the Lord, keep His way, and He shall exalt you to inherit the land, and you will see the wicked cut off.[1]

Remember that every man shall receive his own reward according to his own labor.[2]

115

---

1) Psalms 37:34   2) 1 Corinthians 3:8

116

It is the gift of God for a man to have riches and wealth, to be able to eat and take his portion and to rejoice in his labor,[1] but remember, it is more blessed to give than to receive. [2]

1) Ecclesiastes 5:19   2) Acts 20:35

L et the Lord be magnified which has pleasure in His servants' prosperity.[1]

T he blessing of the Lord makes rich and He adds no sorrow with it.[2]

B y humility and the fear of the Lord are riches and honor and life.[3]

117

1) Psalms 35:27   2) Proverbs 10:22   3) Proverbs 22:4

PROSPERITY

Blessings are upon the head of the just,[1] and a faithful man will abound with them.[2]

In the house of the wise,[3] and the righteous is much treasure to be desired,[4] and oil.[3]

118

1) Proverbs 10:6   2) Proverbs 28:20   3) Proverbs 21:20   4) Proverbs 15:6

PROSPERITY

By knowledge shall the chambers be filled with all precious and pleasant riches.[1] For you know the grace of our Lord Jesus Christ, that though He was rich, yet for your sakes He became poor, that you through His poverty might be rich.[2]

119

1) Proverbs 24:4   2) 2 Corinthians 8:9

PROSPERITY

Those that love wisdom and seek her early, will find her,[1] for she leads in the way of righteousness, in the midst of the paths of judgement,[2] that she may cause you to inherit substance, and she will fill your treasures.[3]

120

1) Proverbs 8:17   2) Proverbs 8:20   3) Proverbs 8:21

PROSPERITY

Did you not know that the wealth of the sinner is laid up for the just?[1] For God gives to a man that is good in His sight, wisdom and knowledge and joy; but to the sinner He gives work, to gather and heap up, to give it to him that is good before God.[2]

121

1) Proverbs 13:22   2) Ecclesiastes 2:26

RESTORATION

Rejoice not against me, O my enemy: When I fall, I will arise: When I sit in darkness, the Lord will be a light to me.[1]

A just man falls seven times, and rises up again,[2] and though he walk in the midst of trouble, God will revive him.[3]

122

1) Micah 7:8   2) Proverbs 24:16   3) Psalms 138:7

RESTORATION

The steps of a good man are ordered by the Lord and He delights in his way; Though he fall, he will not be utterly cast down, for the Lord upholds him with His hand.[1]

123

1) Psalms 37:23,24

RESTORATION

M any are the afflictions of the righteous; but the Lord delivers them out of them all.[1]

F or as the heaven is high above the earth, so great is His mercy toward them that fear Him.[2]

124

1) Psalms 34:19   2) Psalms 103:11

RESTORATION

If we confess our sins, He is faithful and just to forgive us our sins and to cleanse us from all unrighteousness.[1] And He will restore to you the years that the locust has eaten, the cankerworm, and the caterpillar, and the palmerworm.[2]

125

1) 1 John 1:9   2) Joel 2:25

RESTORATION

126

There is therefore now no condemnation to them which are in Christ Jesus, who walk not after the flesh, but after the Spirit.[1] For the Lord will not cast off His people, neither will He forsake His inheritance.[2]

1) Romans 8:1   2) Psalms 94:14

RESTORATION

127

Can a woman forget her sucking child, that she should not have compassion on the son of her womb? Yes, she may forget you, yet the Lord will not forget you,[1] for He has graven you upon the palms of His hands.[2]

128

If a man be overtaken in a fault, you which are spiritual, restore such a one in the spirit of meekness; considering yourself, lest you also be tempted.[1]

The Lord will restore your soul[2] and perfect that which concerns you.[3]

1) Galatians 6:1   2) Psalms 23:3   3) Psalms 138:8

RESTORATION

God didn't send His son into the world to condemn it; but that the world through Him might be saved. He that believes on Him is not condemned.[1]

129

1) John 3:17

130

Cast all your burdens[1] and cares[2] upon the Lord, for He cares for you, and He will sustain you.[1]

Listen to God. Let His peace rule in your heart[3] and you will dwell safely, free from fear of evil.[4]

1) Psalms 55:22   2) 1 Peter 5:7   3) Colossians 3:15   4) Proverbs 1:33

Call upon the Lord in your day of distress, and He will hear you,[1] answer you,[2] redeem your soul,[3] set you in a large place[2] and bring you out of all your distresses.[4]

131

1) Psalms 18:6   2) Psalms 118:5   3) 1 Kings 1:29   4) Psalms 107:28

132

D on't allow your heart to be troubled or afraid[1] and be anxious for nothing, but in everything by prayer and supplication, with thanksgiving, let your requests be made known to God, and the peace of God which passes all understanding will keep your hearts and minds through Christ Jesus.[2]

1) John 14:27   2) Philippians 4:6,7

Remember that God will supply all your needs according to His riches in glory by Christ Jesus,[1] and He will keep you in perfect peace if your mind is fixed on Him.[2]

133

1) Philippians 4:19   2) Isaiah 26:3

D on't give up, for God gives power to the faint and to them that have no might, He increases strength.[1]

W ait upon the Lord to renew your strength, then you will mount up with wings as eagles, run and not be weary, walk and not faint.[2]

1) Isaiah 40:29   2) Isaiah 40:31

Make God your refuge and fortress,[1] placing all your trust in Him[2] and you will live in safety,[3] preserved from trouble,[4] surrounded by mercy,[5] guarded by angels,[6] sheltered from the storm and shaded from the heat.[7]

135

1) Psalm 91:2   2) Psalm 4:5   3) Psalm 4:8   4) Psalm 32:7   5) Psalm 32:10   6) Psalm 91:11   7) Isaiah 25:4

G od is our strength, a very present help in trouble.[1]

136

C all upon Him in the day of trouble. He will come to your defense, be your refuge,[2] hide you in His pavilion, set you upon a rock,[3] calm the storm and bring you to your desired haven.[4]

1) Psalms 46:1   2) Psalms 59:16   3) Psalms 27:5   4) Psalms 107:29,30

During troubled times, God will be with you and honor you,[1] for His thoughts for you are precious, and great is the sum of them.[2]

137

1) Psalms 91:15   2) Psalms 139:17

TEMPTATION

138

There has no temptation taken you but such as is common to man: but God is faithful, who will not allow you to be tempted above that which you are able; but will with the temptation also make a way of escape that you may be able to bear it.[1]

1) 1 Corinthians 10:13

F or this is the will of God, even your sanctification, that you should abstain from sexual immorality.[1]

139

Y ou should know how to control your own body in a way that is holy and honorable, not in passionate lust like the heathen who don't know God.[2]

1) 1 Thessalonians 4:3   2) 1 Thessalonians 4:4

TEMPTATION

Your body is the temple of the Holy Spirit, which is in you as a gift from God.[1]

You are not your own, for you were bought with a price; therefore glorify God in your body and in your spirit which are God's.[2]

140

1) 1 Corinthians 6:19   2) 1 Corinthians 6:20

TEMPTATION

Put on the Lord Jesus Christ, and make no provision for the flesh, to fulfill its lusts,[1] for if you are Christ's then you have crucified the flesh with the affections and lusts.[2]

141

1) Romans 13:14   2) Galatians 5:24

TEMPTATION

142

All that is in the world, the lust of the flesh and the lust of the eyes, and the pride of life is not of the Father, but is of the world.[1] And don't you know that friendship with the world is enmity with God? Whoever is a friend of the world is an enemy of God.[2]

1) 1 John 2:16   2) James 4:4

143

Walk in the Spirit and you will not fulfill the lust of the flesh.[1] Remember, whatever things are true, honest, just, pure, lovely or of good report; if there be any virtue, if there be any praise, think on these things.[2]

1) Galatians 5:16 2) Philippians 4:8

TEMPTATION

144

Watch and pray that you enter not into temptation; for the spirit is indeed willing, but the flesh is weak.[1]

Blessed is the man who endures temptation, for when he is tried, he will receive the crown of life which the Lord promised them that love Him.[2]

1) Matthew 26:41   2) James 1:12

TEMPTATION

L et no man say when he is tempted, "I am tempted of God:" for God cannot be tempted by evil, neither does He tempt any man. But every man is tempted when he is drawn away by his own lust, and enticed.[1]

145

1) James 1:13,14

TEMPTATION

146

When lust has conceived it brings forth sin; and sin when it is finished, brings forth death.[1]

The ways of man are before the eyes of the Lord and He ponders all his goings.[2]

1) James 1:15   2) Proverbs 5:21

TEMPTATION

The Lord knows how to deliver the godly out of temptations,[1] for we have not a high priest which cannot be touched with the feelings of our weaknesses; but was in all points tempted like we are, yet without sin.[2]

147

1) 2 Peter 2:9   2) Hebrews 4:15

148

Y ou can do all things through Christ who strengthens you,[1] because greater is He that is in you than he that is in the world.[2]

W hatever is born of God, overcomes the world, and this is the victory that overcomes the world, even our faith.[3]

1) Philippians 4:13   2) 1 John 4:4   3) 1 John 5:4

WINNING

B e not overcome with evil, but overcome evil with good.[1] To him that overcomes, God will give to eat of the tree of life, which is in the midst of the paradise of God.[2]

149

1) Romans 12:21   2) Revelation 2:7

150

Give thanks to God which always causes us to triumph in Christ,[1] knowing that no weapon formed against you will prosper, and every tongue that rises up against you in judgement, you shall condemn, for this is the heritage of the servants of the Lord.[2]

1) 2 Corinthians 2:14   2) Isaiah 54:17

With God's help you can run through a troop, leap over a wall[1] and triumph in the works of your hands,[2] so run that you may obtain.[3] Thanks be to God which gives you the victory[4] and makes you more than a conqueror through our Lord Jesus Christ.[5]

151

1) Psalms 18:29   2) Psalms 92:4   3) 1 Corinthians 9:24   4) 1 Corinthians 15:57   5) Romans 8:37

WINNING

152

Many are the afflictions of the righteous, but the Lord delivers him out of them all.[1] So clap your hands and shout unto God with a voice of triumph[2] who brings us great victory.[3]

1) Psalms 34:19   2) Psalms 47:1   3) 2 Samuel 23:12

He that wins souls is wise,[1] and you that overcome will be a pillar in the temple of God,[2] be seated with Christ in His throne,[3] inherit all things and be God's son and He will be your God.[4]

153

1) Proverbs 11:30   2) Revelation 3:12   3) Revelation 3:21   4) Revelation 21:7

154

Count all things but loss for the excellency of the knowledge of Christ Jesus, counting everything you lose as dung, that you may win Christ.[1]

1) Philippians 3:8